German – Russian

Favorite Recipes

Volume 3

Reuben A. Bauer
Author

Copyright Page

Heritage Books Canada
ISBN: 978-1-990265-02-0   Printed in Canada

COPYRIGHT © 2021 by Reuben A. Bauer
Author/ Editor: Bauer, Reuben A.

"Old Favorites of the German-Russian Recipes" Volume 3

Summary: This volume, like all the other volumes in this series of Volume 1 to 8, and future ones, are the compilation of good food recipes collected from mothers, grandmothers, and daughters over the centuries past who lived both in the Volga Region of Russia and then migrated to other parts of the world, namely Canada and the United States. Of these forbearers, the descendants are the fortunate ones to inherit a legacy of richness in tasty foods, culture, and history. These recipes are a "must have" to complete the traditions of the past.

First edition published: June 2009
Second edition: November 2009
Third edition: November 2010
Fourth edition: March 2011
Fifth Edition: 2021
Edmonton, Alberta, Canada
Heritage Books Canada
Worldwide distribution:
Heritage Books - Canada, #374, 9768-170 St.,
Edmonton, Alberta, Canada, T5T 5L4

Foreword

In this volume, like all the other seven volumes of the German-Russian Recipes, we see a refreshing selection of old favorite foods that have graced the dinner tables of German-Russian families for decades. Among these collections of "good eating" foods are the recipes that are authentic German dishes. Herein you will also find a sprinkling of other selected and well-used recipes that were favored by the German-Russian families.

All these recipes are the original or derivatives of German-Russian foods. In some cases, modifications have been made from the original recipes to either suit the taste and/or availability of ingredients of the German-Russian housewives, mothers, and grandmothers during the last 250 years plus. In their migration from Germany, these people brought as much with them to settle in their new home along Russia's Volga River region.

We are proud to offer up these authentic and tasty foods in these people's spirits and cultures. Many of these were staple dishes chosen for the week-day eating and the Sunday best by the grandmothers, daughters, and granddaughters in every household. The Volga German-Russian colonists made their home along the Steppes of the Volga River region, often referred to as the "bread-basket" of Mother Russia. The settlement took root as early as 1763 and consisted of 103 colonies.

Join us as we give thanks to God for their lives and their examples to the millions of their descendants worldwide, even to this day. Join us in one of the many prayers of "blessing" that were spoken at the tables before they broke bread and participated in, as well as the prayers of "thanksgiving" offered after eating their delicious and hearty foods.

Throughout this book and all the other eight volumes are the many prayers used in these families' homes in the original German language and translated into English where possible. Accompanying the prayers are some especially fitting proverbs.

TABLE OF CONTENTS

Contents

Soup

FRANZOSEN ZWIEBELSUPPE
(French Onion Soup)

4 onions, sliced

4 Tbsp. butter

2 Tbsp. flour

Dash of Worcestershire sauce

French bread slices, toasted

Grated mozzarella cheese

Parmesan cheese

4 c. beef broth

½ tsp. Salt

½ tsp. pepper

Method:
Sauté onions in butter. Stir in flour and cook for 1 min. Add broth, Salt, Pepper, Worcestershire sauce, and bring to a boil. Reduce heat and simmer 30 min. Heat broiler and put the soup in oven-proof bowls on a baking sheet. Add toast to each bowl and cover with cheese, then broil until brown. (Note: Rub onion soup bowls with cut cloves of garlic. If desired. Yield 4 servings.

RIBBLA SUPPE
(Crumb Soup)

1 c. flour

2 eggs

½ tsp. salt

½ c. water, or less

½ Salt

Method:
Combine 1 cup flour, eggs, and ½ teaspoon salt. Mix by hand until it crumbles into small pieces. A little water may be added as needed. Rub the dough between the fingers to form Ribble. Add salt to taste. Stir in the ribblas.

GERMAN NAVY BEAN SOUP

1½ lb slab bacon, cut into cubes
1 lb. navy beans
½ onion or less
2 - 3 c. diced potatoes

Method:

Wash beans. Fill a 4 -5 qt. Saucepan with water about 2 inches from the top.
Put in bacon, beans, Salt to taste, and onion. Boil slowly for 2 hours to
prevent beans from burning. Add potatoes and cook until done. It should be
nice and thick as the water boils down. If thinner soup is desired, add boiling
hot water with a bit of salt to taste. Very easy to make.

RUSSIAN BORSCHT SUPPE
(Russian Red Beet Soup)

2½ lb. pieces of beef roast (or soup meat)
2 medium potatoes, diced
2 c. red beets, grated or diced
2 bay leaves
1 large onion, sliced
1 pepper, whole (more if desired)

Method:

Use as much water to cover meat and vegetables. Cook 4 to 5 hours slowly.
When ready to serve, remove from the burner, add ½ cup sour cream, or as
much as you like. Serve with German Rye bread.

HUHN UND NOODEL SUPPE MIT FILLZER

(Chicken Noodle Soup with Dressing)

1 egg
1 chicken (nice and plump – 3½ lbs.)
2 Tbsp. butter
2 Tbsp. chopped onion
4 c. dry bread crumbs (more if needed)
½ c. raisins (optional)
½ c. walnuts, crushed (optional)
Milk
Salt to taste

Method:

Melt butter, add onions cook on low heat for about 5 minutes. Pour over bread crumbs, add 1 egg, add enough milk to make crumbs soft. Salt to taste. Let crumb mixture sit and soak up the milk and add more milk if needed. Now add the optional ingredients like raisins and walnuts to the bread crumbs, if desired. Put this crumb mixture inside the chicken and sew up with store string or thread and needle. Place the chicken in a large kettle. Cover with water and add salt and a bay leaf. Cook until tender. Take chicken out and put it into a pan with about ½ cube butter. Brown chicken on all sides. As the chicken is being cooked, you can baste it periodically. Meanwhile, put noodles into boiling broth and cook until tender. Serve with homemade rye bread.

HOMEMADE POTATO SOUP

Leftover mashed potatoes
Onions, minced or, chopped
Butter
Salt
Pepper
Milk

Method:

Take leftover mashed potatoes and heat up. Add some butter and milk. Melt butter in another pan. Then add onions to the mixture and sauté. Add butter mixture to potatoes. Then add Salt and Pepper to taste and add milk and butter to the desired thickness.

GERMAN MUSHROOM SOUP

5 (10 oz.) cans of beef broth
2 c. sliced fresh mushrooms
1 Tbsp. Tomato paste
½ c. dry sherry (optional)

Method:

In a large saucepan, combine beef broth or stock, mushrooms, and tomato paste. Bring to a boil, reduce heat and simmer for 5 minutes or until mushrooms are tender. Stir in sherry, if desired, and serve immediately.

Salads

SŰSSE SAUERKRAUT
(Sweet Sauerkraut)

2 qt. Shredded cabbage
2 large onions sliced
¼ c. Vinegar
¾ c. water
1 Tbsp. Sugar
½ tsp. Salt
1/8 tsp. Pepper

Method:
Cover and cook slowly for 1 hour or more. Then add a little more water if it cooks dry. The more often this dish is reheated, the better it tastes.

VEGETABLE SALAD

1 can peas, drained
1 can carrots, drained
5 tomatoes, cut up
5 cooked potatoes, cut up
5 boiled eggs

Method:
Mix together with Salt, Pepper, and mayonnaise.

TOMATO BASIL WHEAT BERRY SALAD

1 c. wheat berries
8 c. water
¼ c. olive oil
2 Tbsp. White wine vinegar
½ tsp. each Salt and Pepper
2 medium tomatoes, chopped
3 green onions, chopped
¼ c. chopped fresh basil

Method:

Clean and wash wheat berries and then soak in water (to cover wheat berries) for 8 hours. Drain. Add 8 cups water and cook berries on low heat in a covered saucepan until tender (about 90 min.). Drain and cool. Whisk together oil, vinegar, salt, and pepper, pour-over wheat berries. Add tomatoes, onions, and basil. Toss to coat.

CREAM CABBAGE SALAD

2 egg yolks
½ to ¾ c. brown sugar
½ c. cider Vinegar
2 Tbsp. Butter
¼ tsp. Salt
shredded cabbage

Method:

Mix the above ingredients (except cabbage) and bring to a boil. Add a small cup of sweet cream to bring to a boil again. Add butter and salt and pour over shredded cabbage while hot. Do not place it in the refrigerator. Serve salad one hour after making.

GELATIN SALAD

2 (3-oz.) pkg. orange-flavored Jello
1 (16-oz.) can Whole Berry cranberry sauce
12 oz. ginger ale
1/3 c. unsweetened orange juice
1 (8-oz.) can crushed pineapple, undrained

Method:

Combine gelatin and cranberry sauce in a saucepan; stir over low heat until gelatin is dissolved. Stir in ginger ale and juice. Chill until thickened but not set; fold in pineapple. Pour into lightly oiled 5-cup mold. Chill until firm. Unmold onto a serving plate.

DILLED CUCUMBER SALAD

½ c. 1% cottage cheese
¼ tsp. dried dill weed
1 medium onion
½ c. plain non-fat yogurt
¼ tsp. Salt
2 medium cucumbers

Method:

Combine cottage cheese, yogurt, dill weed, and salt in a blender. Blend until smooth. In a small bowl, filled with the mixture, add cucumbers and onions. (Makes about 8 servings – no fat.) 31 calories per servings.

MIXED FRUIT SALAD

½ c. cut pineapple
½ c. diced ripe pears
½ c. grapefruit
½ fresh cherries
1½ c bananas (add ½ tsp. lemon juice to prevent turning dark)
½ c. strawberries
½ c. blueberries
pinch of paprika (or 1/8 tsp.)

Method:

Toss all together lightly with a fork. Chill. Serve with fruit salad dressing on crisp lettuce and melba toast or traditional brown toast. Add a pinch of paprika. Serve.

GERMAN CABBAGE SALAD

2 c. shredded cabbage, fine
1 pimento
1 green pepper
salt
¾ c. shredded pineapple

celery salt
paprika
lettuce, crisp
½ c. salad dressing
1/3 c. chopped celery

Method:

Shred crisp cabbage in cold water. Cut pepper, pimento, mix all ingredients with boiled salad dressing. Add a pinch of paprika.

GERMAN POTATO SALAD

1 qt. diced cold boiled potatoes
4 eggs, hard-boiled, sliced
1 c. celery, hearts cut (let stand in ice water)
½ c. radishes, thinly sliced
1 small onion, cut fine
1/3 c. green peppers, cut fine
1 c. cucumber, diced
1 c. or more salad dressing (or mayonnaise)
celery salt
onion seasoning

Method:

Prepare in the order given. Add paprika before serving. Mix thoroughly, chill, serve on crisp lettuce.

Jemanden Honig umden Mund schmieren

To butter someone up

Main Dish And Casseroles

NEW BREAKFAST CASSEROLE
(Must be prepared day ahead)

5 or 6 slices of bread
1 lb. bulk sausage
8 oz. grated cheddar cheese

Egg Mixture:
6 eggs, beaten well
2 c. milk
1 tsp. Salt
1 tsp. dry mustard

Method:
Cube bread slices into 1½ square pieces and place in one layer at the bottom of the greased 9 x 13-inch pan. Fry and drain sausage. Crumble sausage evenly over the breaded layer. Sprinkle grated cheese evenly over the sausage layer.

Prepare egg mixture:
Beat eggs well; beat in milk, salt, and dry mustard. Drizzle egg mixture evenly over the bread, sausage, and cheese layers. Cover the pan with aluminum foil and allow it to sit overnight in the refrigerator. Bake in 350*F oven for 1 hour in the morning, leaving it covered with foil. Serves 6 generously.

CHICKEN POT PIE

Method:
Boil chicken in salt and pepper water. Reserve 1 soup can full of broth. Use 2 to 3 cups cooked chicken.

Mix all together:
1 small bag of frozen vegetables
Onion flakes
1 can cream of chicken soup (do not dilute)
Pat of butter
Cook 5 medium-sized potatoes, peeled.

Method:
Add broth a little at a time. Do not make it too soupy. Put 5 medium-cooked potatoes mashed on top. Cook all this together and put it in a deep baking dish. And place in the oven long enough to brown and serve.

QUICHE LORRAINE
Short crust pastry

Filling:
4 oz. chopped bacon or ham
3oz. cheese, thinly sliced
2 eggs
$\frac{1}{4}$ pt. milk
Salt and pepper to taste

Method:
Line a 7-inch shallow round baking tin with the pastry. Fry the bacon lightly; allow to cool. Place the cheese in the pastry case and cover it with bacon. Beat the eggs and milk together, season, and pour over the cheese and bacon. Bake in a moderate oven at 375*F until set and golden brown, about 40 minutes.

WIENER SCHNITZEL
Old fashioned German Recipe (This is a straightforward method.)

1-2 egg yolks, beaten
flour
very thin veal slices
Salt and Pepper
fine bread crumbs
butter
lemon slices (optional)

Method:
If the veal is not cut very thin, pound it a little. Add some seasoning to beaten egg yolks. Dip veal slices in Flour, then in egg yolks, then in breadcrumbs. As veal slices are thin, cook only a few minutes in hot butter until golden on both sides. Serve immediately on a hot dish. Garnish with lemon slices if desired.

CHICKEN & RICE CASSEROLE

1 can cream of chicken soup
1 can cream of mushroom soup
1 c. raw rice (uncooked)
½ c. water
1 box Lipton Onion soup

Method:
Mix ingredients thoroughly in an 8 x 9 x 2-inch baking dish and place chicken on top. Sprinkle with Lipton Onion soup. Salt and pepper to taste. Bake at 350*F for 2 plus hours.

CHILI MEATBALLS

1 lb. ground beef
2 Tbsp. bread crumbs
milk to soften

2 Tbsp. onion (or onion powder)
1 Tbsp. chili powder

Sauce:
1 can tomato soup
1/3 c. water
1 Tbsp. chili powder
1 clove garlic, minced

Method:
Simmer the entire mixture for 20 minutes and then serve.

CHEESEBURGER CASSEROLE

1 lb. ground beef
1 c. Minute rice, uncooked
1 can tomato soup
1 medium onion, chopped
1 tsp. salt
1/8 tsp. pepper
1 Tbsp. Worcestershire sauce

Method:
Brown the meat and onions in an ungreased skillet. Add all remaining ingredients and mix well. Put mixture into a casserole dish and cover with sliced cheese, then top it off with canned biscuits making sure that the biscuits cover the ingredients. Bake in an oven at 350*F. for about 20 minutes.

SWEET 'N SOUR FRANKS

1 can tomato soup
¼ c. grape jelly
1 lb. wieners, cut into 1-inch pieces
1 can (20 oz.) pineapple chunks, drained.
1 Tbsp. mustard
¼ c. vinegar

Method:

In a saucepan on medium heat, put soup, jelly, vinegar, and mustard. Heat until jelly melts, and the mixture is very warm. Then add pineapple and wieners.

PORK BALLS AND SAUERKRAUT

2 c. cooked pork, ground
½ c. rice uncooked
1 qt. Sauerkraut
½ tsp. Salt
¼ tsp. Pepper

Method:

Mix pork and rice, then add salt and pepper and form into small balls. Spread half of the sauerkraut in the bottom of a casserole dish. In this place, add the meatballs and top with the rest of the kraut. Bake at 350*F. then cover and bake for 1 hour. It serves a family of 4

HASHED BROWN POTATOES

3 potatoes, enough to make 4 c.
1 - 2 Tbsp. Grated onions
1 tsp, Salt
dash of pepper
¼ c. butter

Method:

Take 3 potatoes, cook them in their jackets, peel, shred onto waxed paper to make 4 big, pressed cups. Mix in 1 to 2 tablespoons of grated onion, 1 teaspoon salt, and a dash of pepper. In a 10-inch skillet, heat ¼ cup butter or drippings, add potatoes, pat down, leaving ½ inch space for fat to bubble around the edges. After cooking for 8 to 10 minutes, check for brownness, reduce heat if necessary. Brown for additional 8 to 10 minutes longer till the crust is golden brown. Served with scrambled eggs and sausages. Garnish with tomato slices and parsley.

NOODLES AND POTATOES

Boil homemade noodles (This and That)section in the back of this book on "Making Homemade Noodles From Scratch"). Boil noodles in salt water for 20 minutes. Add cubed boiled potatoes. To taste, put in a casserole, brown slightly, combine with melted butter and bread crumbs, and pour over noodles.

OVEN-FRIED CHICKEN

1 c. cut-up fryer

1 egg, beaten

1/3 c. cream

1 small onion, diced

¼ c. cream

1 c. rolled cornflakes

½ c. dry bread crumbs

paprika

garlic salt

Method:

Combine beaten egg and ¼ cup cream. Then season to taste. Dip cut pieces of chicken into egg mixture and roll in cornflakes and bread crumb mixture. Lay chicken in a flat open buttered pan. Dot with butter and paprika and onion, and bake at 400*F for 25 minutes. Turn and bake until golden brown. Then baste with 1/3 cup cream and bake 10 minutes more. Serve hot.

FILLED LUNCHEON BUNS

½ lb. cheddar cheese, grated

3 or 4 green onions, chopped

1 large tomato, chopped

2 hard-boiled eggs, chopped

½ can of ripe olives, chopped

½ c. tuna fish

Salt, pepper to taste

Mayonnaise

Method:

Mix all ingredients with a fork. Take part of the middle out of 1½ dozen oblong rolls and fill with mixture. Wrap individually in aluminum foil and heat in the oven about ½ hour before serving at 350*F.

KRAUT KUCHEN (OLD STYLE)
Cabbage Bread

Beef meat	2 onions
1 c. milk scalded	1 large head cabbage
1 c. potato water	1 egg
1 tsp. Salt	2 Tbsp. sugar
2 pkg. yeast	7 c. Flour

Method:

Boil some beef; let cool and cut fine. Fry onions and cabbage till done, not brown over low heat, and stir continually. Season to taste, mix with meat. Scald the milk and cool. Soak yeast in little warm water and mix all ingredients into the medium dough. Let rise and work down twice. Take a small portion-sized dough about the size of an orange and roll out to about ¼ inch thickness. Put 2 large tablespoons of meat-cabbage mixture filling into each center of the laid-out dough. Pinch the ends and across the top tightly. Lay in baking pan face up and brush with butter and let rise for about 10 minutes. Then put them in the oven at 350*F for about 35 minutes. Be sure to use more cabbage than meat. (Some village families used only cabbage and no meat. (This choice is optional). This will be a meal in itself with coffee or tea. These also taste delicious cold, or they may be heated up at a later time. Leftovers should be stored in the refrigerator or you may freeze them for use later.

Es ist nicht alles Gold was glanzt

Everything that glitters isn't Gold

Breads

APRICOT NUT BREAD

2 Tbsp. melted butter
1 egg, slightly beaten
1 c. milk
2 c. sifted Flour
3 tsp. Baking powder
½ tsp. Salt
½ tsp. Baking soda
1 c. sugar
¾ c. finely chopped dried apricots
½ c. chopped walnuts
1½ tsp. grated lemon rind

Method:

Preheat oven to 350*F, moderate. Grease a 9x5x3 inch loaf pan. Sift together flour, baking powder, salt, baking soda, and sugar. Stir in apricots, nuts, and lemon rind. Add melted butter, egg, and milk, all at once, and stir only enough to moisten dry ingredients. Do not beat. Turn into prepared pan. Bake for 1 hour.

PFFERNEUSS

1 c. sugar
1/3 c. Wesson oil
2 eggs beaten

1 tsp. Pepper or ginger

2 c. water
¾ c. molasses
1 Tbsp. Salt
1 cake yeast
1 tsp. Cinnamon
8 c. Flour

Method:

Dissolve yeast in 1/4 cup warm water with 1 tsp. sugar. Beat the eggs and sugar; add salt, molasses and water, and yeast. Add dry ingredients which have been sifted together. Add 1/3 cup Wesson oil last. Knead until smooth. Let rise 1½ to 2 hrs. Knead dough down twice. Form biscuits place side by side. Let rise again 45 minutes to 1 hour. Bake 45 minutes at 300°F.

AIR BUNS

1 pkg. yeast
1 tsp. Sugar
½ c. warm water
Soak yeast in water for 10
minutes.
9 c. Flour

2 tsp. Salt
½ lb. lard, melted
½ c. sugar
1 Tbsp. Vinegar
4 c. water

Method:

Make a well in the Flour. Add remaining ingredients. Stir with a spoon. Knead dough. Cover and let rise 2 times. Shape into buns and bake.

HOMEMADE BREAD

7¼ c. white Flour

2 pkg. dry yeast

3 Tbsp. Sugar

1 tsp. Salt

4 tsp. shortening

2 c. hot water

¼ c. lukewarm water

Method:

Combine sugar, salt, and shortening with hot water; let it cool. Combine yeast and lukewarm water to dissolve yeast. Combine the above ingredients; add Flour; mix and knead until smooth. Cover the bowl and let rise about 4 hours until it doubles in size; punch down and make into 2 loaves. Bake in 425*F oven for 30 minutes.

VESS MARIA'S CORNBREAD
(Aunty Mary's Cornbread- Norka Colony)

2 c. self-rising Flour (white)

1 c. self-rising cornmeal

1½ c. milk

3 Tbsp. butter, melted

2 eggs

Method:

Heat oven to 425*F. Mix flour, cornmeal, slightly beat egg and milk. Add to flour and meal mixture. Add butter and mix well. Pour into a square pan (buttered). Bake 25 to 30 minutes until done, golden brown. Brush tops of bread with butter after baking

DEENA KUCHEN

(Coffee Cake)

Making of sweet dough for Deena kuchen

SWEET DOUGH

2 c. lukewarm milk

½ c. sugar

2 tsp. Salt

7-7½ c. Flour sifted

2 compressed yeast cakes

2 eggs

½ c. soft shortening (or ¾ c. butter)

Method:

Mix milk, sugar, and salt together; crumble the yeast cakes into the mixture. Stir until yeast is dissolved; stir in eggs and shortening. Mix in first with a spoon, then with hands by adding the Flour. Add Flour in two parts, using the amount necessary to make it easy to handle. Cover and let rest for 15 minutes. Work dough down and let rise until light (15 to 30 minutes). Roll out for coffee cake. Let rise and bake as for Apfel Kuchen or Kaese Kuchen. Using a sweet roll dough (as above), roll dough to fit the bottom of a square pan or rectangular pan. Spread the following mixture on top of Kuchen

Method:

Cream this well with a mixer, add 1 whole egg, beat in well, and add 1 tablespoon flour. A small amount of cream, about 2 tablespoons, may be added if the mixture is thick. Sprinkle with Rival Topping.

Rival Topping:

½ c. Flour	½ c. sugar
¼ c. butter	

Work these ingredients into a crumb mixture, spread over the dough, and bake in the oven for 35 minutes at 350*F.

6 – WEEKS BRAN MUFFINS

1 (15-oz.) box raisin bran flakes

3 c. sugar

5 c. Flour

5 tsp. Baking soda

2 tsp. Salt

4 eggs, beaten

1 qt. buttermilk

1 c. salad oil

Method:

Combine and refrigerate in a covered container. These muffins can be stored for 6 weeks, if need be. Bake the desired amount from the batter at a 400*F temperature for 12 to 15 minutes and then serve.

ORENGA MUFFINS

(Orange Muffins)

3 Tbsp. Butter

½ c. light brown sugar

2 eggs

2 c. flour sifted

1 orange, juice, and rind

1 c. milk

4 tsp. Baking powder

¼ tsp. Salt

Method:

Sift flour, baking powder, and salt. Then blend in with melted butter, beaten eggs. Mix with milk, make a smooth batter. Add orange juice, rind. Bake in greased muffin tins for about 20 minutes in the oven at about 425*F.

SPICE MUFFINS
(Gewürzmuffins)

2/3 c. butter

1 c. sugar

3 eggs (whites and yolk – separated)

1 c. molasses

1/3 tsp. Salt

1 c. sour milk

½ tsp. Cinnamon

½ tsp. Nutmeg

½ tsp. Baking soda

3 c. flour, sifted

2 tsp. Baking powder

Method:
Mix cream and butter, then beat and add in sugar. Add egg yolks and molasses. Sift dry ingredients, add alternately with milk. Add beaten egg whites. Fill buttered tins two-thirds full. Bake about 20 minutes in a 425*F oven.

Jemanden Honig umden Mund schmieren

To butter someone up

Rolls

POTATO ROLLS

1 c. hot mashed potato
1¼ c. potato water
1 egg
5 c. sifted all-purpose Flour
½ c. shortening
½ c. sugar
1½ tsp. Salt
1 cake of compressed yeast

Method:

Mix together potatoes, potato water, and shortening. Cool to lukewarm; dissolve in it 1 cake yeast. Add sugar, egg, 1 cup flour, and salt. Mix thoroughly and set in a warm place to rise for 20 minutes. Add 4 cups flour; knead until smooth and elastic. Let rise until doubled in bulk (about 2 hours). Shape into rolls and place in greased pans. Let rise until double; bake at 400*F for 15 to 20 minutes. Brush rolls with soft butter before baking with 2 teaspoons of sugar dissolved in ¼ cup milk.

Das Brot das Leben

Bread of Life

BUTTERHORNS
(Butterhörner Kuchen)

1 cake compressed yeast

1 c. lukewarm water

1 c. milk

6 Tbsp. sugar

1½ tsp. Salt

6 Tbsp. shortening

1 egg

6 c. enriched Flour, sifted

Method:

Soften yeast in lukewarm water. Scald milk and add sugar, salt, and shortening. When lukewarm, add 1 cup flour and beat thoroughly. Add egg and yeast and beat well. Add enough more flour to make a soft dough. Knead until smooth and satiny. Grease bowl around side; cover and let rise in a warm place until doubled in bulk. Then knead down again and let rise. Take portions of dough and roll to ¼ inch thickness. Put in a pie pan or cake pan and let rise for about 15 minutes. Put on custard, about 2 or 3 tablespoons to a pie tin.

Custard

1 c. sour cream

1 egg

1 Tbsp. sugar

Pinch of Cinnamon

Method:

Mix ingredients well. Put about 2 to 3 tablespoons into each pie tin. Add any kind of fruit and another tablespoon or more sugar, and a tiny pinch of cinnamon. Bake for 15-20 minutes at 375*F.

SWEET ROLLS

1 cake yeast
¼ c. lukewarm water
1 Tbsp. sugar
½ c. oil
1 ¼ tsp. Salt

1 c. scalded milk
½ c. sugar
3 eggs, beaten slightly
3 c. Flour

Method:
Combine yeast, 1 tablespoon sugar, and lukewarm water. Mix well. Add sugar, oil, salt to scalded milk and cool. Add beaten eggs and yeast to cool milk. Add flour and mix thoroughly. Make a soft dough. Put the dough in a greased bowl. Brush with oil, cover, and chill, and then let rise 3 times, kneading each time. Make rolls and bake 15 minutes at 350*F. (If you wish, before baking, you could twist them in a spiral.)

KRATZ KOCHA
(A Scratch Biscuit – Norka Village)

1 c. sweet cream
2 eggs
1 ½ tsp. Salt
1 Tbsp. sugar
1 c. Flour (or more for a soft dough like a biscuit)

Method:
Mix like biscuit dough and cut into small squares approximately 5" x 3". Put slits in them with a sharp knife and bake in oven 400*F until brown. Serve with jam, peanut butter using fresh butter. They taste and look like a biscuit. Very good.

Bleena

NORKA BLINZEE
(Norka Crepes)

3 eggs
½ tsp. Salt
¼ c. water

1 c. Flour
1¼ c. milk
2 Tbsp. butter

Method:
Beat eggs with Salt, add Flour with liquid ingredients. Mix well and add melted butter. Let stand 1 hour at room temperature. Pour into a greased frying pan, turning once. Fill with fruits, jam, peanut butter, or whatever topping you desire. You may also like to use whipped cream or syrup.

Mann denkt aber Gott lengkt

Man thinks but God leads

RUSSIAN BLINI
(Russian Style Crepes)

1½ c. lukewarm milk

1 cake compressed yeast

2 c. fine buckwheat Flour

4 egg yolks

½ tsp. Salt

1 Tbsp. sugar

1½ c. lukewarm milk

2 tsp. butter

4 egg whites, beaten stiff

Method:
Pour warm milk over crumbled yeast. Stir to dissolve and add about 1 cup flour to make a thick sponge. Heat a cloth, cover the bowl and stand in a warm place for about 2 ½ hours. Beat egg yolks with salt and sugar, stir into additional warm milk, and add melted butter. Combine with the raised sponge. Mix in remaining flour and egg whites. Cover again and all mixture to stand for at least 20 minutes. Heat skillet and bake small pancakes not larger than 3 inches across. Next, brown slightly on both sides. These can be served first with melted butter and salted herring, caviar, or melted butter and sour cream. Makes 30 blini.

Other Version:
It is possible to make and use the same ingredients but bake in a cast-iron skillet, lightly brown on both sides, stack, with each blini spread with a small amount of melted butter or fat. Keep in a warm oven until ready for serving. Serve with melted butter; preserves, syrups, whipped cream, sour cream, desserts, or first course, with meats like link sausages, fish, not sweets.
A second or third choice for a spread on these blini is the use of peanut butter topped with liquid Honey.

Pancakes

APFEL PANNE KUCHEN
(Apple Pancakes)

4 eggs
½ c. milk
½ tsp. Salt
2 Tbsp. sugar
2 c. Flour

3 LG. apples, sliced thin
3 tsp. Cinnamon
½ c. sugar
3 Tbsp. butter

Method:

Beat eggs until <u>very</u> thick. Add milk, salt, and sugar; beat. Sift in flour; mix well. Let batter stand for 30 minutes. Butter <u>well</u> a 9 x 13-inch pan. Prepare apples, peeled and sliced thin. Sprinkle the bottom of the pan with part of the cinnamon and sugar mixture. Arrange apples in the pan. Sprinkle with remaining cinnamon and sugar and dot with butter. Pour batter over apples. Bake at 375*F for 30 minutes. Serve with maple syrup, whip cream, or ice cream.

Menchen essen aber Ferden fressen

People eat, but animals gobble

SOUR MILK GRIDDLE CAKES

2 eggs, yolks, whites beaten separately

2 c. sour milk

2½ c. flour, sift, then measure

3 tsp. Baking powder

2 Tbsp. Granulated sugar

½ tsp. Baking soda

4 Tbsp. Butter, melted over hot water

½ tsp. salt

Method:

Sift together dry ingredients. Add sour milk and beaten egg. Have griddle hot, syrup hot, platter hot. Use a soapstone griddle *(which should never be washed but cleaned thoroughly with Salt and keep the skillet in a covered bag when not in use. Try using a half cup of salt in a clean thin white bag, rub the salt bag back and forth over the skillet after each baking).* Beat egg yolks separately, add flour mixture alternately with milk. Just before baking, add butter and fold in stiffly beaten egg whites. For thick cakes, use 1 to 1½ cups of milk.

KARTOFFEL PUFFER MIT APFFELMUS
(Potato Pancakes with Applesauce)

6 medium potatoes, raw
and grated fine

2 beaten eggs

¼ c. finely grated onion

¼ c. Flour

1 tsp. Salt

bacon fat or lard for
frying

Method:

Mix all ingredients well, adding each at a time. Fry pancakes over moderate heat for about 2 minutes on each side to a golden brown with crisp edges. Serve with preserves, peanut butter, or fruit.

Cakes (Kuchen)

GRAMMA'S DELICIOUS GINGERBREAD

1 c. brown sugar
½ c. Crisco shortening or margarine
2 eggs
¾ c. molasses (light)
2 ¾ c. sifted Flour
2 tsp. Baking soda
2 tsp. ginger (more if needed)
1 tsp. Cinnamon
½ tsp. Salt
1 c. buttermilk or sour milk
Ice cream, whipped cream, or applesauce

Method:

Blend sugar, shortening, and eggs. Stir in molasses. Add combined dry ingredients alternately with buttermilk or sour milk (made with 1 tablespoon vinegar to 1 cup milk); beat well. Spread in a well-greased and floured 13 x 9 x 2-inch pan. Bake at 350*F for 30 to 40 minutes. Serve warm with ice cream, whipped cream, or applesauce. Serves 8 to 10.

KAISER'S FAVORITE COFFEE CAKE

3 eggs
1 c. sweet cream
½ c. sweet milk
3 tsp. Baking powder

dash of a star of anise
½ c. lard, melted
¾ c. sugar
1 tsp. Salt

Method:

Flour enough to make a soft dough. Mix with a spoon. Take a small amount and roll on floured board. Put in a greased pie tin. Top with topping like fruit and custard or sour cream and brown sugar and cinnamon or rieval. Serves about 6.

ICEBOX CAKE
(A Family Favorite)

1 1/3 c. sugar

3 eggs, beaten

2 Tbsp. cornstarch

2 c. milk

1 lb. Vanilla wafers, crushed

½ pt. whipped cream

Method:

Cook together over a slow fire or in a double boiler until thick as for custard. Let cool; put a layer of crumbs, then the custard, then crumbs, etc. Top with whipped cream.

OUR FAVORITE DEENA KOCHA

(Our Favorite Crumb Cake)

2 c. brown sugar

1 c. shortening

4 c. Flour

2 tsp. Cinnamon

1 tsp. cloves

1 c. raisins

2 c. sour milk

2 tsp. Baking soda

Method:

Crumble together brown sugar, shortening, and Flour. Keep ½ cup of the mixture back to sprinkle over the cake before baking. Add ½ cup water to raisins; bring to boil and drain. Put raisins in crumb mixture. Add sour milk, baking soda, cinnamon, cloves. Bake 375*F until done. Bake for about 45 minutes in an 8 x 12-inch pan.

Alles hat eine Ende, nur die Wurst hat zwei

Everything has an end, on the sausage has two

Cookies (Gaschnickker)

Gaschnickker (German-Russian Volga term used to describe Desserts, Sweets, Pies, Cookies, etc....... the afterglow to the main course)

OATMEAL COOKIES

½ c. butter or margarine
½ c. shortening softened
1 c. brown sugar
1 tsp. Baking soda
¼ tsp. Vanilla
1 c. Flour
1 egg
2½ c. oatmeal

Method:

Cream butter and shortening. Add brown sugar, egg, and vanilla; beat until light. Stir in flour, baking soda, and rolled oats. This dough can be chilled in rolls, sliced and baked, rolled in balls, and pressed with a fork. Bake on an ungreased cookie sheet at 350* F. for 12 to 15 minutes.

SALTED PEANUT COOKIES

1 c. white sugar

1 c. brown sugar

1 c. shortening

2 eggs

1 c. peanuts, salted

1 tsp. Baking soda

1 tsp. Baking powder

2 c. oatmeal

2 c. Cornflakes

1 tsp. Vanilla

2 c. Flour

Method:

Cream the shortening, both kinds of sugars, and eggs. Add dry ingredients. Then blend in oatmeal, salted peanuts, and Cornflakes. Roll into balls and bake at 350* F.

BANANA ROLLED OATS COOKIES

Bananen-Hoverflocken-Kekse

$1\frac{1}{2}$ c. sifted Flour

1 c. sugar

$\frac{1}{2}$ tsp. Baking soda

1 tsp. Salt

$\frac{1}{4}$ tsp. Nutmeg

$\frac{1}{2}$ c. chopped nuts

$\frac{3}{4}$ tsp. Cinnamon

$\frac{3}{4}$ c. shortening

1 egg well beaten

1 c. mashed ripe bananas

$1\frac{3}{4}$ c. rolled oats

Method:

Sift together flour, sugar, soda, Salt, nutmeg, and cinnamon. Cut in butter or shortening. Add eggs, bananas and rolled oats, and nuts. Beat until thoroughly blended. Drop by tablespoons about 1½ inches apart onto a lightly floured sheet. Bake in 375°F oven for about 10 to 12 minutes.

MAPLE WALNUT CREAMS

¾ lb. maple sugar

3 Tbsp. Boiling water

½ c. cream

¾ c. chopped walnuts

1 tsp. maple flavoring

Method:

Boil sugar, water, and cream to the softball when tested in cold water. Remove from heat; add nuts and flavoring and beat until creamy. Bake at 375* until brown.

Kommt last uns Betten

Let us give thanks

DATE FILLED COOKIES

¾ c. butter
1½ c. Flour sifted
1½ c. quick oatmeal

1 c. brown sugar
4 Tbsp. milk
1 tsp. Baking soda
2 tsp. Baking powder, level

Method:
Blend all ingredients like pie crust. Roll thin on lightly floured board cut with a round cookie cutter, place teaspoon of date filling on a cookie, cover with dough and bake in the oven for 375*F.

FILLING:

1 c. granulated sugar
1/3 tsp. Vanilla
1 pkg. dates (remove stones and cut)
1 c. water.

Method:
Combine ingredients and cook this mixture until thick and cool, then add flavoring.

PRUNE DESSERT

1 cup chopped prunes
Whipping cream

1 cup chopped walnuts
1 tsp honey

Method:
Pit the prunes which have been soaked overnight. Mix walnuts with chopped prunes and serve with whipped cream and Honey

Desserts

APPLE DELIGHT
(Apfel Freude)

2 eggs
2 c. sugar
½ c. shortening
2 c. Flour
2 tsp. Baking soda
1 tsp. Cinnamon

1 tsp. Nutmeg
½ tsp. Salt
1 c. chopped nuts
2 c. chopped or grated apples

Method:
Beat eggs, sugar, shortening until creamy. Add apples, then dry ingredients and nuts. Mix well. Bake in 350*F oven for 40 minutes using a 9 x 13-inch pan. Serve with sauce or whipped cream.

Sauce:
½ c. butter
½ c. cream

1 c. sugar

Method:
Bring to boil, add 1½ tsp. of Rum or vanilla. Serve this sauce hot over the dessert.

ANGEL FOOD DELIGHT

This mixture makes a large angel food cake
Make a custard in a double boiler; cook until it coats spoon:

6 beaten egg yolks
6 beaten egg whites
¾ c. lemon juice
¾ c. sugar
1½ tsp lemon rind grated
1/8 tsp. Salt
1 Tbsp. Gelatin
¼ c. cold water

Method:
Grease angel cake pan. Remove from heat; add 1 tablespoon gelatin in ¼ cup cold water. Beat 6 egg whites separately until stiff and then fold in ¾ cup sugar. Fold into custard. Break cake into chunks and press in a pan with layers of custard. Let stand overnight. Frost with whipped cream before serving.

Dank Gott für alles Essen

Thank God for all our food

ICEBOX PUDDING

2 egg yolks

$\frac{1}{2}$ lb. Vanilla wafers

$\frac{1}{4}$ lb. butter

$\frac{3}{4}$ c. sugar

$1\frac{1}{4}$ c. chopped walnuts

1 can crushed pineapple, crushed

Method:

Cream butter and sugar, add egg yolks. Add crushed pineapple and ¾ cup nuts. Line the baking dish with a layer of wafers. Add a layer of the above mixture, then wafers, until you have 3 layers of wafers with a mixture between and on top. Cover with remaining nuts. Chill 15 hours. Serve with whipped cream and maraschino cherries.

CHERRY CHEESE DESSERT

1 $\frac{1}{2}$ c. graham cracker crumbs

1 $\frac{1}{4}$ c. melted butter

$\frac{1}{4}$ c. granulated sugar

1 (8 oz.) Philadelphia cream cheese

$\frac{1}{2}$ c. powdered sugar (another name- icing sugar)

$\frac{1}{2}$ tsp. Vanilla extract

$\frac{1}{2}$ tub (8-oz.) Cool Whip

1 can cherry pie filling

Method:

Combine graham cracker crumbs and granulated sugar with melted butter, press into an 8 x 8-inch pan, and chill. Beat cream cheese until fluffy. Add powdered sugar and vanilla extract and beat until smooth. Fold the Cool Whip into the cream cheese mixture and stir until well blended. Spoon the cream cheese mixture onto the chilled crust. Spoon the cherry pie filling evenly over the cream cheese layer. Refrigerate 2 hours before serving. Before serving, add a dollop of whipped cream or Cool Whip to each serving.

Pies

PUMPKIN PIE ALASKA

10 large marshmallows

1 c. pumpkin

2/3 c. brown sugar

$\frac{1}{4}$ c. orange juice

$\frac{1}{2}$ c. whipped cream

$\frac{1}{4}$ tsp. Salt

$\frac{1}{4}$ tsp. Ginger

$\frac{1}{2}$ tsp. Cinnamon

4 egg yolks beaten

9" pie shell

Method:

Partially melt marshmallows over hot water. Blend in pumpkin, sugar, and Salt. Combine ginger and cinnamon and stir into marshmallows. Blend in orange juice; remove from heat. Blend ½ cup of mixture with beaten egg yolks. Combine with the remaining hot mixture, beat vigorously. Return to double boiler and cook 3 to 4 minutes, stirring constantly. Remove from heat; chill. Fold whipped cream into the mixture.

Put as much ice cream as you like in a cooled pie shell about ½ inch thick and freeze. Spoon pumpkin mixture over ice cream and freeze until firm. At serving time, swirl mile-high meringue over frozen pie. Be sure to seal the meringue to the edge of the crust. Bake in a very hot oven 475*F. for 3 to 5 minutes, until meringue is lightly browned. Remove from oven and serve at once.

MILE HIGH MERINGUE

4 egg whites
½ c. sugar
¼ tsp. cream of tartar

Method:

Beat egg whites and cream of tartar until frothy. Gradually add sugar, a tablespoon at a time, beating constantly. Continue beating until stiff and glossy. Swirl on a pie.

RITZ CRACKER PIE

3 egg whites
½ tsp. Baking powder
1 c. sugar
17 cheese Ritz Crackers, finely crushed
2/3 c. chopped walnuts (coarse)

Method:

Beat egg whites until frothy. Add baking powder and beat until stiff. Gradually add sugar and continue beating. Fold in cracker crumbs, then nuts. Pour into butter 8-inch pie pan and bake 35 minutes at 350*F. Cool and serve with whipped cream. If made with plain Ritz Crackers, add vanilla flavoring.

GERMAN LEMON PIE

1½ c. sugar

1/3 c. sifted Flour

2 c. boiling water

pinch of Salt

4 egg yolks, beaten

4 Tbsp. corn starch

1 Tbsp. butter

6 Tbsp. lemon juice

2 tsp. grated lemon rind

1 baked pie shell

Method:

Blend the cornstarch, flour, and sugar. Stir, and add to boiling water. Stir constantly for about 5 minutes, cover mixture, and steam for 15 minutes. Add butter and beaten egg yolks together, cook for only 2 minutes. Remove from heat, add lemon juice, and grated rind. When cool, fill baked pie shell, cover with meringue. (See "This and That" in the back of the book for making meringue or use the recipe below).

Meringue:

2 egg whites, beaten stiff

3 Tbsp. Sugar

½ tsp. Lemon juice

¾ tsp. Vanilla

Method:

Cover the top of the pie and return to the oven to lightly brown. For thick meringues, bake in the slow oven between 300 to 325* F for 20 to 30 minutes depending upon thickness until there will be no syrupy liquid around the edge of the pie.

Grebbles

Each family and village had their own special kind of Grebble and ingredients to match. (Grebles, Grebbel, Grebbles, Krepple were a type of German-Russian doughnut. The spelling of the word differed from village to village.)

BAUER GREBBEL
(Bauer Family Deep Fried Donuts)

3 eggs
2 tsp. Baking powder
1-pint sour whipping cream
½ c. sugar
1 tsp. Salt
¼ tsp. Cloves
½ tsp. Baking soda
4-5 cups Flour

Method:

Beat eggs, add sugar, beat mixture. Add the rest of the ingredients and mix well. Add enough flour to make a soft dough. Roll on floured board to 1/4 inch thickness. Cut in 2½" x 4" squares. Make 2 slits in each, pull one corner thru the opposite slit. Fry in deep fat until nice and brown. Optional, sprinkle or roll with sugar. (*Commonly baked in the Villages of Bauer and Norka.*)

RUSSIAN GREBBLE

2 cans of milk
1 yeast cake
¼ c. warm water
2/3 c. butter
1 Tbsp. Salt
5 eggs beaten
4 tsp. Baking powder heaping
½ c. sugar
1 Tbsp. Vanilla
Use about 5 c. Flour

Method:

Cook the milk and let stand. Then take the yeast soaked in warm water. Add the butter into the hot milk and let cool. When cool, mix the yeast and the milk. Add a tablespoon of salt and the well-beaten eggs, add 4 teaspoons of baking powder, a half cup of sugar, and one tablespoon of vanilla, and stir. As you are stirring, add enough flour to make a soft dough. Let rise 3 times and beat it down each time. Then roll ou the dough gently with your hands. This should be a soft dough. Cut them in 2 x 3-inch strips. Then cut a slit in each piece of dough. Fry in deep oil and sprinkle with sugar.

KŰCHLE GREBBLES

1 pt. sour cream
1½ Tbsp. sugar
1½ tsp. Baking powder
½ tsp. Vanilla
3 eggs

1½ tsp. Baking soda
dash of Salt (1/8 tsp.)
flour enough to make a
soft dough

Method:

Mix the cream, sugar, and baking powder. Add eggs, baking soda, salt, and vanilla in that order. Add Flour. Roll out and cut in squares about 3" x 3". Make two slashes diagonally. Draw one corner through one slash. Drop into hot grease and brown on both sides. Roll in powdered sugar and serve hot, warm, and fresh.

OLD-FASHIONED DOUGHNUTS

2 c. Flour (self-rising)
1/8 tsp. Nutmeg
2 Tbsp. Crisco shortening
½ c. sugar
1 egg, beaten
½ tsp. Vanilla
1/3 c. buttermilk

Method:

Sift Flour; add nutmeg; resift twice. Cream shortening; blend in sugar thoroughly. Add beaten egg and vanilla. Add the dry ingredients and buttermilk alternately, stirring only until well mixed. Chill dough before rolling. Using a lightly floured board, roll out and cut with a floured cutter. Fry in deep fryer heated to 375*F. Fry until golden brown on both sides. Lift out; drain on paper towels. (Roll in granulated sugar, 4X sugar or cinnamon, and sugar/walnuts, if desired.)

STRAUBER GREBBLES

(Village of Straub—favorite Doughnuts)

1 Tbsp. butter	½ c. cream
1 egg	5 tsp. Baking powder
3 egg yolks	½ c. milk
1 c. sugar	1 tsp. Salt
4 c. Flour sifted	½ tsp. Nutmeg

Method:

Cream butter and sugar together, beat in egg, then beat in yolks, one at a time. Stir in milk gradually, then cream and nutmeg. Sift dry ingredients together and stir into sugar mixture, blending well. Roll on a lightly floured board using a doughnut cutter with a hole in the center. Fry in hot, deep fat, 360-370*F for 2 to 3 minutes, turn on both sides to get a consistency of golden brownness and remove from frying as soon as they rise to the top. Remove, place on unglazed paper to drain. Use sugar to dip in and chopped walnuts for extra flavor. Reheat in a covered casserole dish or top of a double boiler over hot water before serving.

Das sind meine Grebbles

Those are my grebbles

Glösse (Dumplings)

(Glösse, Glace, Glees, Gleese, Kleasel, Glöessé, Klösse were the different spellings for this word. Each family and village had their own special kind of Dumplings and ingredients to match. The spelling of the word differed from village to village.) The Glosse were used as a garnish with soups, like rice, potato, and noodle soups. Various fruits were also put into dumplings.

COTTAGE CHEESE DUMPLINGS

1 lb. dry cottage cheese
9 Tbsp. flour
4 eggs
½ c. bread crumbs
2 Tbsp. butter
pinch of Salt

Method:

Put cheese through a strainer; add beaten eggs. Stir and add Flour and Salt. Mix until smooth. Form into balls with moist hands. Drop-in boiling saltwater, boil 25 minutes or less. Remove with a slotted spoon to remove water in the process; roll in buttered crumbs. Serve hot.

Ich brauche mehr!

I need more!

GERMAN GLACÉ

Method:
Peel and cube 1 large potato. Boil in a large kettle in 2 quarts of water and 1 tablespoon salt. Boil until almost done, then spoon in glace. Use a tablespoon, dipping spoon in hot water after each glace. Bring to a full rolling boil, drain and either fry them or brown bread crumbs in butter and pour over glacé and potatoes. Also, pour light cream over glacé.

Glacé dough:
1 c. Flour

1 egg

½ tsp. Baking powder

½ tsp. Salt

¼ c. milk

Method:
Mix with a spoon until well blended. Spoon out pieces the size of a peanut. Glace will swell up.

EGG DUMPLINGS

1 c. Flour

1 tsp. Baking powder

pinch of Salt (1/8 tsp.)

3 eggs, beaten

½ c. milk (approximately)

Method:
Make a stiff enough dough to hold shape. Add eggs and milk to Flour, Salt, and baking powder. Drop by tablespoonful into boiling water, to which a pinch of salt has been added. Boil just long enough for dumplings to rise to the top. Drain well. Brown onions in butter or margarine in a frying pan, pour over dumplings and serve.

KARTOFFEL UND GLEES
(Potatoes and Dumplings)

3-4 potatoes, peeled and
quartered
1 egg
bread crumbs

3 heaping Tbsp. Flour
½ cube butter, melted
1 c. hot cream

Method:

Boil potatoes in 4 quarts of salted water. When half done, add flour, egg, and a little water to make a thick batter. With a teaspoon, drop each dumpling in with potatoes and boil for 15 minutes or until done. Dough may be made as stiff as soft noodle dough and cut with a knife. Drain and garnish with melted butter, bread crumbs, and hot cream. Serve.

Last mehr machen!

Lets make more!

THIS AND THAT

German-Russian ladies in the homemade kitchens did not have store-bought vanilla. There were no corner grocery stores, like we have today, to which they could go and buy this ingredient for baking. They had to make their own brand of vanilla. Here is how to make your own vanilla.

HOMEMADE VANILLA

1 Vanilla bean, chopped
½ tsp. sugar
3 oz. Vodka

Method:

Put in a jar, cover tightly, shake well every day for a month. It is then ready to use.

FRUIT SYRUP for WAFFLES AND PANCAKES

1 c. brown sugar
½ c. corn syrup
1 c. fruit juice

Method:

Boil 3 minutes. Add your favorite canned fruit diced. Serve hot.

TOPPING WITH MERINGUE

$\frac{1}{4}$ tsp. Cream of tartar

4 Tbsp. Sugar

2 egg whites

$\frac{1}{2}$ tsp. Vanilla

Method:

Now be prepared to whip first of all the 3 ingredients until soft peaks form. Gradually add sugar until all is dissolved and the meringue is glossy. Bake at 350*F. for 12 – 15 minutes. (For a more enormous amount of meringue, use 3 egg whites and 6 Tbsp. of sugar.

MAKING "RIEVAL" TOPPINGS FOR COFFEE CAKES

1 c. Flour

1 cube butter, melted in saucepan

$\frac{1}{2}$ c. sugar

Method:

Add flour and sugar to butter with hand or spoon. Mix until the coarse, crumbly mixture develops. This becomes the topping used on almost all German Coffee Cakes.

HOW TO MAKE CHOCOLATE CANDY

1 lb. milk chocolate
1 c. broken walnut pieces
½ lb. fresh marshmallows

Method:

Melt chocolate in a double boiler over warm water. (Water should be no hotter than is comfortable to the hand) Stir occasionally into an 8 inch greased pan, cut marshmallows. Sprinkle nuts over marshmallows and mix thoroughly. When chocolate is melted (about 45 minutes later), pour over the other mixture. Allow standing 6 to 8 hours yields about 1 ¾ pound of candy.

CANDIED WALNUTS

1½ c. sugar
½ c. water
¼ c. Honey
½ tsp. Vanilla

Method:

Stir and boil to 245*F on a candy thermometer or softball stage. Remove from heat; add ½ teaspoon vanilla and 3 cups crisp walnut halves (or cashews, peanuts, almonds, etc.). Stir until thick and creamy, pour into greased pan. Separate with 2 forks. Makes 1½ pounds. (Cinnamon or grated orange rind may be added.)

PASCKA (Russian)
(Especially for Easter)

4 large pkg. Philadelphia cream cheese

¼ c. butter (1 cube), melted

½ c. sour cream

1 c. candied fruit, chopped fine

4 Tbsp. sugar

1 pkg. Chopped almonds

½ c. raisins

Method:

Mix the above ingredients well, adding one at a time. Shape mixture into a pyramid-like mold to become firm. To keep moist and drying out, place a wet cheesecloth into the mold before putting it in the mixture. This pyramid-like box is upside down like a **V** shape. The mixture is poured in from the wide end. Place in a refrigerator to keep cool. Place some heavyweights on the pascka, which is in the frame, so it will sit nicely. Before removing the frame, place it on your favorite big plate (right-side up), remove the wooden mold or frame, and then remove the cheesecloth. Some families would decorate the pascka with tiny pieces of colorful Easter candy eggs or chocolate chips. Then serve.

Usually, this pascka was prepared a day or two ahead of Good Friday, so it was ready to eat on Good Friday and throughout the Easter weekend, including Easter Sunday.) (This mold was usually handmade with ¼" plywood or boards with a symbol carved on each inside frame: cross, ladder, egg, and tree. These symbols had special meaning for the church family. The cross signified the death of Christ, the ladder signified the Ressurection of Christ, the egg signified the new life and rebirth in Christ. The tree symbolizes the "tree of life" that God gave mankind to grow and be fruitful and multiply.

PASKA (German)

(Especially for Easter Celebration)

3 lbs. dry cottage cheese

½ lb. butter

1¼ c. sugar

1 c. whipping cream or (thick farm cream)

3 egg yolks

½ tsp. Salt

1 tsp. Vanilla (or rum flavoring)

1 c. white raisins (or dark raisins)

¾ c. mixed candied fruit (optional)

Method:

Put cottage cheese through a ricer. Have butter at room temperature. Beat cream with a fork until frothy. Thoroughly mix cottage cheese, butter, eggs, cream, sugar, salt, and flavoring. Add raisins and fruit. Put into wooden form. (See description above.) If the form is not available, punch a hole in the bottom and side a 2-pound coffee can. Line the container with cheesecloth and fill it to the top. Put a small plate on top so it will fit inside the can. Weigh down with a heavy bottle, medium-sized rock, or jar filled with water. Set into the refrigerator for 24 hours. Unmold and serve.

(Prayers like these in the German language were said at mealtimes.)

Das Blut' Jesus Christus
Macht uns rein
Von allen Sünden. Amen.

The blood of Jesus Christ
Will purify us
From all our sins. Amen

MAKING HOMEMADE NOODLES FROM SCRATCH

(This recipe for making homemade egg noodles was done in Norka and Odessa villages, which were sent to us by descendants of those communities.)

3 eggs, beaten
2 Tbsp. milk
2 c. white Flour
1 tsp. Salt

Method:

Combine all ingredients and mix well. (May require more milk than this.), to make a stiff dough. Roll very thinly. Roll up the dough, as you would for a jelly-roll, and then cut noodles from the roll with a sharp knife. Before cutting the dough roll, let it stand in a covered bowl with a tea towel for an hour. Then roll. Cutting each roll very thinly at an angle, pressing with one hand on the roll to keep it firm until all are cut. To help dry the noodles, toss them up and fluff to let them air out. When sufficiently dry, place them in a plastic bag and put them in the refrigerator for an hour or longer for use in soups or casseroles. Be prepared to put them into a chicken broth, ready for the soup.

Sind da mehr?

Is there more?

HOW TO MAKE "BAKING POWDER BISCUITS"

2 c. Flour sifted

4 tsp. Baking powder

½ tsp. Salt

4 Tbsp. butter (or another shortening)

¾ c. milk

Method:

Sift flour, measure, add salt, baking powder, and sift again. Cut in shortening (butter), gradually add milk, and make into a soft dough. Roll one-half-inch thickness with little Flour on board, cut with a floured biscuit cutter, and bake in a hot oven for about 15 minutes at 450*F.

Aber das Schmecht sehr gut!

But that tastes really good!

BENEFITS OF HONEY AND CINNAMON

As we know, Honey (in its natural form) is a food source that does not spoil. The German-Russians used Honey and cinnamon, nutmeg, paprika, and cayenne pepper with great frequency in their cooking and ordinary medicines. As the grandmothers did most of the cooking and baking, and the daughters and daughters-in-law were busy raising and nurturing their children, the grandmothers knew all these old recipes and remedies for health and survival.

As you will see in many German-Russian recipes, Honey is a substitute for sugar as a sweetening agent. Besides, cinnamon was used so frequently in cooking and baking as a natural seasoning. The health benefits that these ingredients had were genuinely marvelous.

We have taken this for granted in the latter years and largely ignored these remedies as old-fashioned and "old wives tales". I have taken the liberty to give you the age-old remedies used by the grandmothers down through the ages with great success. Many current studies now reveal that these old recipes and remedies are more valuable, practical, and beneficial for health and survival than previously thought. As modern-day medicines were unknown and unavailable to many of these German-Russian people.

It is found that a mixture of Honey and Cinnamon cures most of the diseases. Honey is produced in most of the countries of the world. German-Russians have been using these mixtures of Honey and other seasonings as a vital medicine for centuries as a cultural group. Scientists of today also accept Honey as a beneficial medicine for all kinds of diseases. Honey can be used without any side effects for any kind of disease. Today's science says that even though Honey is sweet if taken in the proper dosage as a medicine, it does not harm diabetic patients.

HEART DISEASES: Make a paste of honey and cinnamon powder, apply on bread, toast, or other bread, instead of jelly and jam and eat it regularly for breakfast. It reduces the cholesterol in the arteries and saves the patient from a heart attack. Those who already had an attack can also keep miles away from the next attack if they do this process daily.

Regular use of the above process relieves loss of breath and strengthens the heartbeat. In the United States and Canada, various nursing homes have treated patients successfully and have found that as they age, the arteries and veins lose their flexibility and get clogged; Honey and cinnamon revitalize the arteries veins.

INSECT BITES: Take one part honey to two parts of lukewarm water and add a small teaspoon of cinnamon powder, make a paste, and massage it slowly on the itching part of the body. It is noticed that
The pain recedes within a minute or two.

ARTHRITIS: Arthritis patients may take daily, morning and night, one cup of hot water with two spoons of Honey and one small teaspoon of cinnamon powder. If taken regularly, even chronic arthritis can be cured.

In recent research conducted at the Copenhagen University, it was found that when the doctors treated their patients with a mixture of one tablespoon Honey and half teaspoon Cinnamon powder before breakfast, they found that within a week out of the 200 people so treated, practically 73 patients were totally relieved of pain and within a month, mostly all the patients who could not walk or move around because of arthritis started walking without pain.

HAIR LOSS: Those suffering from hair loss or baldness may apply a paste of hot olive oil, one tablespoon of Honey, one teaspoon of cinnamon powder before bath, and keep it for approx. 15 min. and then wash the hair. It was found to be useful even if kept on for 5 minutes.

BLADDER INFECTIONS: Take two tablespoons of cinnamon powder and one teaspoon of Honey in a glass of lukewarm water and drink it. It destroys the germs in the bladder.

TOOTHACHE: Make a paste of one teaspoon of cinnamon powder and five teaspoons of Honey and apply it on the aching tooth. This may be applied 3 times a day till the tooth stops aching.

CHOLESTEROL: Two tablespoons of Honey and three teaspoons of Cinnamon Powder mixed in 16 ounces of tea water, given to a cholesterol patient, was found to reduce the cholesterol level in the blood by 10% within 2 hours. As mentioned for arthritic patients, if taken 3 times a day, any Chronic cholesterol is cured. As per information received in the said journal, pure Honey taken with food daily relieves cholesterol complaints.

COLDS: Those suffering from common or severe colds should take one tablespoon lukewarm Honey with 1/4 spoon cinnamon powder daily for 3 days. This process will cure most chronic coughs, colds and clear the sinus.

INFERTILITY: German-Russian grandmothers often used this honey mixture to strengthen the semen of men. If impotent men regularly take two tablespoons of Honey before sleeping, their problem will be solved.
Today in China, Japan, and Far-East countries, women, who do not conceive and need to strengthen the uterus, have been taking cinnamon powder for centuries. Women who cannot conceive may take a pinch of cinnamon powder in half a teaspoon of Honey and apply it on the gums frequently throughout the day. It slowly mixes with the saliva and enters the body.

UPSET STOMACH: Honey taken with cinnamon powder cures stomachache and also clears stomach ulcers from the root.

GAS: According to the studies done in India & Japan, it is revealed that if Honey is taken with cinnamon powder, the stomach is relieved of gas.

IMMUNE SYSTEM: Daily use of honey and cinnamon powder strengthens the immune system and protects the body from bacteria and viral attacks. Scientists have found that Honey has various vitamins and iron in large amounts. Constant use of Honey strengthens the white blood corpuscles to fight bacteria and viral diseases.

INDIGESTION: Cinnamon powder sprinkled on two

tablespoons of Honey taken before food relieves acidity and digests the heaviest meals.

INFLUENZA: A scientist in Spain has proved that Honey contains a natural ingredient, killing the influenza germs and saving the patient from flu.

LONGEVITY: Tea made with honey and cinnamon powder, when taken regularly, arrests old age ravages. Take 4 spoons of Honey, 1 spoon of cinnamon powder, and 3 cups of water and boil to make like tea. Drink 1/4 cup, 3 to 4 times a day. It keeps the skin fresh and soft and arrests old age. Life span also increases, and even a 100-year-old starts performing the chores of a 20-year-old.

PIMPLES: Three tablespoons of Honey and one teaspoon of cinnamon powder paste. Apply this paste on the pimples before sleeping and wash it the following day with warm water. If done daily for two weeks, it removes pimples from the root.

SKIN INFECTIONS: Applying Honey and cinnamon powder in equal parts on the affected parts cures eczema, ringworm, and all types of skin infections.

CANCER: Recent research in Japan and Australia has revealed that the stomach and bones' advanced cancer have been cured successfully. Patients suffering from these kinds of cancer should take one tablespoon of Honey daily with one teaspoon of cinnamon powder for one month, 3 times a day.

FATIGUE: Recent studies have shown that the sugar content of Honey is more helpful than being detrimental to the body's strength. Senior citizens, who take Honey and cinnamon powder in equal parts, are more alert and flexible.

Dr. Milton, who has done the research, says that a half tablespoon honey is taken in a glass of water and sprinkled with cinnamon powder, taken daily after brushing, and in the afternoon at about 3.00 p.m. when the vitality of the body starts to decrease, increases the vitality of the body within a week.

BAD BREATH: People of South America, first thing in the morning, gargle with one teaspoon of honey and cinnamon powder mixed in hot water. So their breath stays fresh throughout the day.

HEARING LOSS: Daily morning and night, Honey and cinnamon powder taken in equal parts restore hearing.

*NOTE: The Honey used needs to be **REAL RAW UNPASTEURIZED HONEY**. If it says PURE Honey, it has most likely been pasteurized.

It is best to only **buy Honey that says RAW or UNPASTEURIZED** on the label. The difference is that the enzymes are all lost when heated out of the pasteurized Honey.

CINNAMON & HONEY WEIGHT LOSS FORMULA :

This should be prepared at night before going to bed.

1. Use 1 part cinnamon to 2 parts raw Honey. 1/2 tsp cinnamon to 1 tsp honey is recommended but can be used more or less as long as in the ratio of 1 to 2.... so 1 tsp. Cinnamon to 2 tsp. Raw Honey is ok too, as an example.

2. Boil 1 cup...that is 8 oz of water.

3. Pour water over cinnamon and cover, and let it steep for 1/2 hour. (30 minutes)

4. Add Honey now that it has cooled. Never add Honey when hot, as the heat will destroy the enzymes and other nutrients in the raw Honey.

5. Drink 1/2 of this directly before going to bed. The other 1/2 should be covered and refrigerated.

6. In the morning, drink the other half that you refrigerated...but do not reheat it...drink it cold or at room temperature only.

Do not add anything else to this recipe. No lemon, no lime, no vinegar should be added. It is unnecessary to drink it more times a day...it is only effective on an empty stomach and primarily at night.

This works for most people. Inches are lost before any measurement on the scales. This program will cause significant inches lost...but you will reach a plateau and may not lose anymore. This is because the cinnamon and Honey cause a cleansing effect in the digestive tract and cleans out parasites and other fungus and bacteria that slow down the digestion...causing a toxic build-up. (Lowers pH) Once this is all cleaned out, then you will most likely have the weight loss slow down.

Other side effects from a cleansing can occur because of toxins being released...if this occurs, cut back on how much you use or take a break.

Additionally, people report increased energy, more sex drive, and feeling happier/mood enhancers.

****

For Additional works by Reuben Bauer please explore our website:

Readthepast.ca

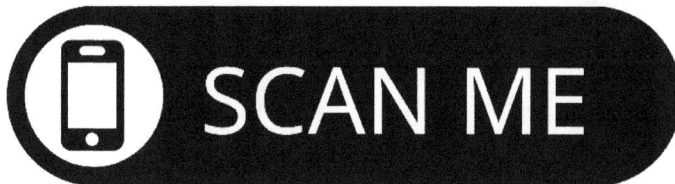

www.ingramcontent.com/pod-product-compliance
Lightning Source LLC
Chambersburg PA
CBHW062115090426
42741CB00016B/3424